はしがき

　この免震装置は、縦・横揺れの地震に対応したものであり、横揺れの場合に於ては建物が元の位置に戻り、縦揺れの場合に於いても、元の位置に戻るものである。

　この作用効果の構成・構造は耐久性を有し、連続揺れの地震に対応でき、また、コスト面に於いても、低コストで提供できる。

　本書では、特許の明細書で表現できない所をカラーのイラスト（斜視、断面）、を用いて、分かり易いように著作権表現で解説した。これにノウハウの一部を追加し、同様に解説した。

Preface

Quake-absorbing equipment returns to the origin position also in a vertical earthquake.

Quake-absorbing equipment returns to the origin position also in a horizontal earthquake.

The composition and structure of quake-absorbing equipment have durability, and can respond also in a continuation earthquake.

Quake-absorbing equipment can be offered at low cost.

In this book, copyright expression explained the place which cannot be expressed on patent specifications.

A part of know-how was added to this, and it explained similarly.

目 次

1、縦・横揺れの免震装置（イラスト解説）

(1) 一部断面を表す斜視図 ·· 5
(2) 地震・振動前の状態の断面 ·· 6
(3) 地震・振動時の断面 ·· 7
(4) 連続地震・振動時の断面 ··· 8
(5) 地震・振動時、横揺れの断面 ······································ 9
(6) 緩衝材使用の地震・振動前の状態の断面 ·····················10
(7) 緩衝材使用の地震・振動時の断面 ·······························11
(8) 緩衝材使用の連続地震・振動時の断面 ························12
　　　本書の奥付の発行No.について ···································47

English of the usage

2、

In-every-direction quake-absorbing equipment

(1)··13

The perspective diagram which expresses a section in part

(2)··14

The section of the state before an earthquake and vibration

(3)··15

The section at the time of an earthquake and vibration

(4)··16

The section at the time of a continuation earthquake and vibration

(5)··17

It is the section of width swing at the time of an earthquake and vibration.

(6)··18

The section of the state in front of the earthquake of the material use which absorbs vibration

(7)··19

The section in case of the earthquake of the material use which absorbs vibration

(8)--20

The section in case of the continuation earthquake of the material use which absorbs vibration

3、公報解説--21

4、Patent journal English---44

    About issue [of the colophon of this book] №----------------------------47

1、縦・横揺れの免震装置（イラスト解説）

(1) 一部断面を表す斜視図

上部構造物には、柱、梁などがボルトで固定される。

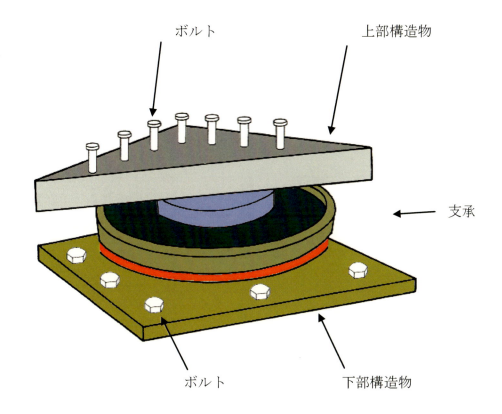

上部構造物と下部構造物の間に縦・横の振動エネルギーを免震する支承が設けられている。

下部構造物は基礎部にボルトで固定される。

※宣伝・説明・明細書表現などへの引用を禁止。

(2) 地震・振動前の状態の断面

支承の弾性円形板材が凹状に湾曲した状態である。

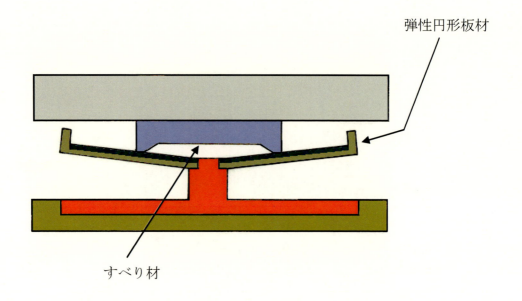

地震・振動前の状態では、すべり材の位置は、弾性円形板材の凹状の湾曲弾性作用により、湾曲した中央にある。

※宣伝・説明・明細書表現などへの引用を禁止。

(3) **地震・振動時の断面**

地震時に上部構造物の荷重で弾性円形板材の凹状の湾曲から平板状態になる。

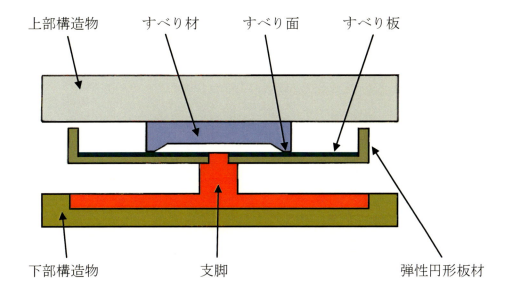

この平板状態になった時点から縦揺れの場合と、横揺れの場合の振動エネルギーにより、すべり材が任意の方向に可動される。

※宣伝・説明・明細書表現などへの引用を禁止。

⑷ 連続地震・振動時の断面

平板状態になった時点から縦揺れの場合において、連続縦揺れは弾性円形板材が下向きに湾曲した形状の状態になる。また、減衰作用の状態となる。

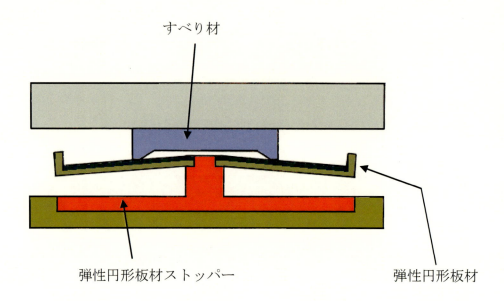

下向きに湾曲した弾性円形板材の降下エネルギーを受け止める弾性円形板材ストッパーが設けられ、下向きに湾曲した弾性円形板材は平板状・上向き湾曲に戻る弾性作用を有している。

※宣伝・説明・明細書表現などへの引用を禁止。

⑸ **地震・振動時、横揺れの断面**

横揺れの振動エネルギーを弾性円形板材で緩和し、すべり材・すべり板で免震する。

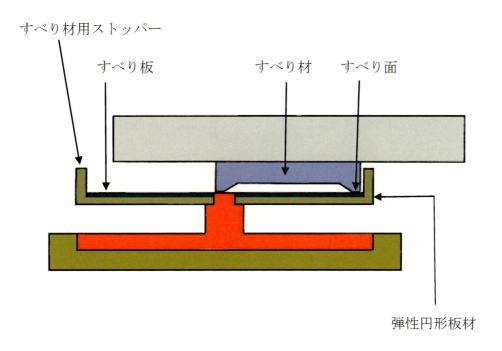

縦揺れ、横揺れの複雑な地震、振動に対して、弾性円形板材の弾性作用によるすべり材・すべり面の免震可動ですべり材は、すべり材用ストッパーで制御される。

※宣伝・説明・明細書表現などへの引用を禁止。

⑹　緩衝材使用の地震・振動前の状態の断面

前記⑵の断面で解説した免震装置にノウハウに一部を追加して、解説する。弾性円形板材と弾性円形板材ストッパーの間に緩衝材を設ける。

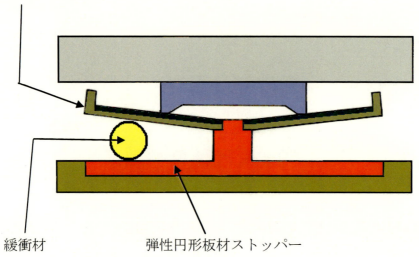

緩衝材に於いては、球状、立方体、直方体、リング状、平板状などの物が、上部構造物の負荷重により、選択される。例えば、軽量鉄骨、重量鉄骨、鉄筋コンクリートなどの建物により、緩衝材の個数が選択される。

※宣伝・説明・明細書表現などへの引用を禁止。

(7) **緩衝材使用の地震・振動時の断面**

前記(3)の断面で解説した免震装置にノウハウに一部を追加して、解説する。弾性円形板材と弾性円形板材ストッパーの間に緩衝材を設けた緩衝材が地震により、上部構造物の負荷が緩衝材にも及び緩衝材が変形する。

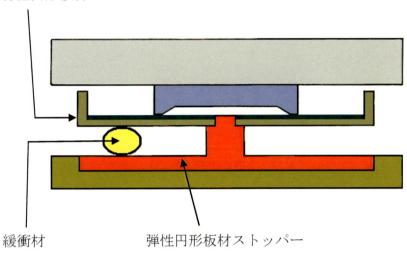

弾性円形板材

緩衝材　　　弾性円形板材ストッパー

緩衝材は上部構造物の負荷により、変形するものと、或いは、変形しないものがあり、その選択は、上部構造物の負荷内容により異なる。

※宣伝・説明・明細書表現などへの引用を禁止。

(8) 緩衝材使用の連続地震・振動時の断面

前記(4)の断面で解説した免震装置にノウハウに一部を追加して、解説する。

前記、(7)から更に上部構造物の負荷が緩衝材にも及び緩衝材が楕円に変形する。

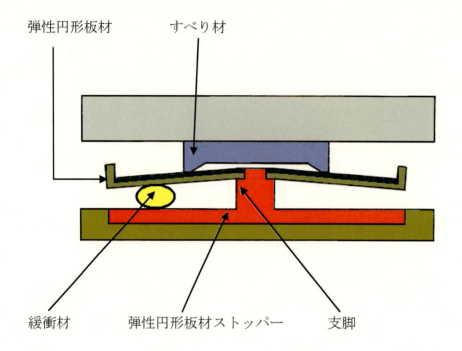

楕円に変形した緩衝材から更に連続的な地震・振動のエネルギーは、支脚と緩衝材との間の弾性円形板材にすべり材から負荷される。

※宣伝・説明・明細書表現などへの引用を禁止。

2、

In-every-direction quake-absorbing equipment

(1)

The perspective diagram which expresses a section in part

A pillar, a beam, etc. are fixed to an up structure with a bolt.

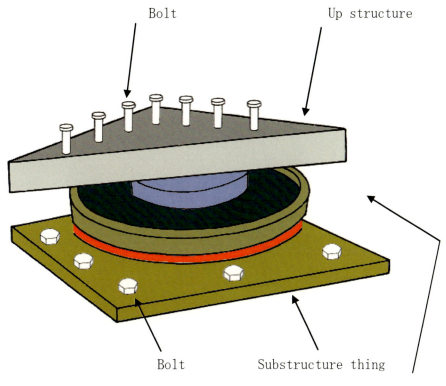

It carries out quake-absorbing [of the oscillating energy in every direction] between an up structure and a substructure thing.

A substructure thing is fixed to a basic part with a bolt.

The quotation to advertisement, explanation, specification expression, etc. is forbidden.

(2)

The section of the state before an earthquake and vibration

Elastic round shape board material is in the state which curved to the concave.

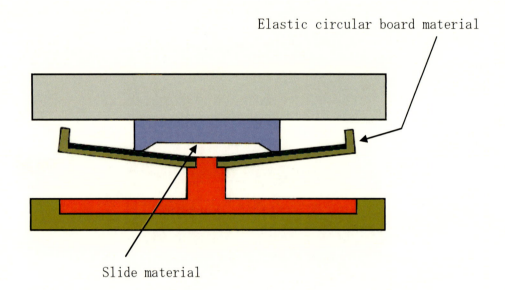

In the state before an earthquake and vibration, there is a position of slide material in the curved center by the concave curve elastic action of elastic round shape board material.

The quotation to advertisement, explanation, specification expression, etc. is forbidden.

(3)

The section at the time of an earthquake and vibration

It will be in a monotonous state from the concave curve of elastic round shape board material by the load of an up structure in case of an earthquake.

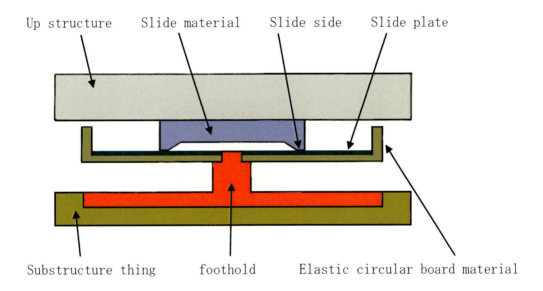

After being in this monotonous state, slide material is moved in the arbitrary directions by oscillating energy in every direction.

The quotation to advertisement, explanation, specification expression, etc. is forbidden.

(4)

The section at the time of a continuation earthquake and vibration

After changing monotonously, a continuation local earthquake becomes the form where elastic round shape board material curved downward.

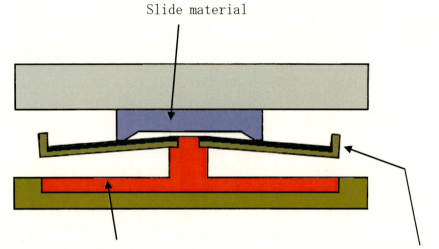

Slide material

Elastic circular board material stopper   Elastic circular board material

The elastic round shape board material stopper which catches the earthquake energy of the elastic round shape board material which curved downward is formed, and the elastic round shape board material which curved downward has the elastic action which returns to the shape of a plate, and a upward curve.

The quotation to advertisement, explanation, specification expression, etc. is forbidden.

(5)
It is the section of width swing at the time of an earthquake and vibration.

Oscillating energy is eased by elastic round shape board material, and it carries out quake-absorbing by slide material and the slide plate.

The stopper for slide material
Slide plate   Slide material   Slide side

Elastic circular board material

The slide material by the elastic action of elastic round shape board material is controlled by the stopper for slide material to the complicated earthquake of an every direction shake.

The quotation to advertisement, explanation, specification expression, etc. is forbidden.

(6)

The section of the state in front of the earthquake of the material use which absorbs vibration

A part is added and explained to the quake-absorbing equipment explained in the section of the above 2 at know-how

Shock absorbing material is prepared between elastic round shape board material and an elastic round shape board material stopper.

Elastic circular board material

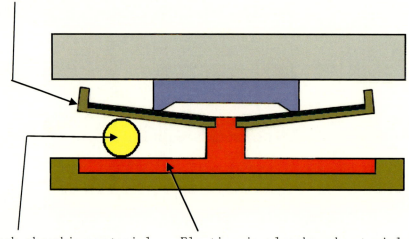

Shock absorbing material   Elastic circular board material stopper

The shape of the shape of a globular shape, a cube, and a ring and a plate etc. has shock absorbing material, and it is chosen by the weight of an up structure.

For example, the number of shock absorbing material is chosen by buildings, such as a weight steel frame and ferro-concrete.

The quotation to advertisement, explanation, specification expression, etc. is forbidden.

(7)

The section in case of the earthquake of the material use which absorbs vibration

According to an earthquake, elastic round template material and the shock absorbing material which prepared shock absorbing material among elastic round template material stoppers reach and transform the load of an up structure also into shock absorbing material.

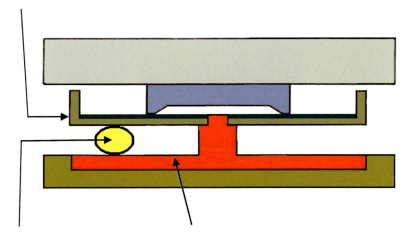

Elastic circular board material

Shock absorbing material   Elastic circular board material stopper

what Shock absorbing material transforms by the load of an up structure -- or there are some which are not transformed and the selection is based on the weight of an up structure

The quotation to advertisement, explanation, specification expression, etc. is forbidden.

(8)

The section in case of the continuation earthquake of the material use which absorbs vibration

A part is added and explained to the quake-absorbing equipment explained in the section of the above 4 at know-how.

The load of an up structure also attains to shock absorbing material further from the above 7, and shock absorbing material changes into an ellipse.

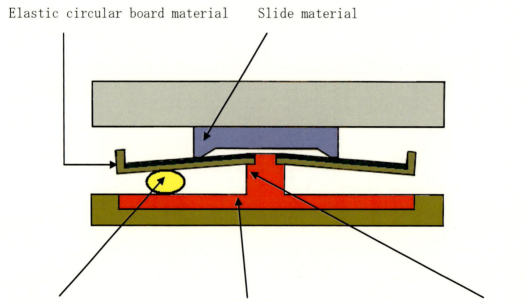

Elastic circular board material   Slide material

Shock absorbing material   Elastic circular board material stopper   foothold

Load of the energy of a continuous vibration is carried out to the elastic round shape board material between foothold and shock absorbing material from slide material from the shock absorbing material which changed into the ellipse.

3、公報解説

特許第5662923号

発明の名称；免震装置

特許権者；佐山　光男

【特許請求の範囲】

【請求項1】

　上部構造物と下部構造物との一方にすべり材が固定され他方にすべり板が固定されたすべり支承構造を備えた免震装置において、すべり板はすべり材に向けて中心部から凹状に湾曲するように付勢され非免震動作時に上部構造物の荷重で平板状になるように弾性が設定された円板形の板材で形成され中心部でのみ部分的に支脚によって支持されて固定され、すべり材はすべり板にリング状に当接されるすべり面が設けられていることを特徴とする免震装置。

【請求項2】

　請求項1の免震装置において、すべり板は円板形の本体部の周縁にすべり材側に突出されすべり材の滑動域を規制するすべり材用ストッパが設けられていることを特徴とする免震装置。

【請求項3】

　請求項1または2の免震装置において、すべり板が固定された上部構造物または下部構造部にすべり板のすべり材と反対側方向への弾性変形域を規制するすべり板用ストッパが設けられていることを特徴とする免震装置。

【発明の詳細な説明】

【技術分野】

【0001】

　本発明は、上部構造物と下部構造物との間に設備されて上部構造物，下部構造物の一方から他方へ伝わる震動（振動）を減衰する免震装置に係る技術分野に属する。

【背景技術】

【0002】

　免震装置としては、すべり支承構造を備えたものが普及している。この免震装置

は、上部構造物，下部構造物の一方にすべり材が固定され他方にすべり板が固定され、すべり材をすべり板に沿って滑動させることで、上部構造物，下部構造物の一方から他方へ伝わる震動を減衰するものである。

【０００３】
　この免震装置では、横方向の震動に対して有効に減衰機能を発揮するものの縦方向の震動に対してほとんど減衰機能を発揮しないという特性がある。このため、すべり支承構造を備えた免震装置において縦方向の震動に対しても有効に減衰機能が発揮される技術の開発が要望されている。

【０００４】
　従来、すべり支承構造を備えた免震装置において縦方向の震動に対しても有効に減衰機能を発揮させることを指向した技術としては、例えば、特許文献１に記載のものが知られている。

【０００５】
　特許文献１には、上部構造物にすべり板が固定され、下部構造物に蛇腹形の空気ばねを介してすべり材が固定され、下部構造物に空気ばねの伸縮方向を規制するガイドシャフト，リニアブッシングからなるガイド機構が取付けられた免震装置が記載されている。

【０００６】
　特許文献１に係る免震装置は、空気ばねによって縦方向の震動に対して減衰機能を発揮させるとともに、すべり材，すべり板からなるすべり支承構造の基本構成を維持して横方向の震動に対する減衰機能が消失しないようにするものである。

【先行技術文献】
【特許文献】
【０００７】
【特許文献１】特開平１０－１６９７０８号公報
【発明の概要】
【発明が解決しようとする課題】
【０００８】
　特許文献１に係る免震装置では、縦方向の震動に対して減衰機能を発揮する空気

ばねを有効に動作させるためにガイド機構の付設が必要とされることから、構造が複雑化して設備コストが高くなってしまうとともに、大きな荷重が掛かり細小な機構の付設が不向きな大型の構造物に適用することができないという問題点がある。

【0009】

本発明は、このような問題点を考慮してなされたもので、横方向，縦方向の双方の震動に対して減衰機能を発揮することができて、設備コストが安価であるとともに大型の構造物に適用することのできる免震装置を提供することを課題とする。

【課題を解決するための手段】

【0010】

前述の課題を解決するため、本発明に係る免震装置は、特許請求の範囲の各請求項に記載の手段を採用する。

【0011】

即ち、請求項1では、上部構造物と下部構造物との一方にすべり材が固定され他方にすべり板が固定されたすべり支承構造を備えた免震装置において、すべり板はすべり材に向けて中心部から凹状に湾曲するように付勢され非免震動作時に上部構造物の荷重で平板状になるように弾性が設定された円板形の板材で形成され中心部でのみ部分的に支脚によって支持されて固定され、すべり材はすべり板にリング状に当接されるすべり面が設けられていることを特徴とする。

【0012】

この手段では、すべり支承構造を構成するすべり材に弾性を付与することで、すべり材自体に縦方向の震動に対する減衰機能を発揮させ、特許文献1に係る免震装置のガイド機構を不要にする。また、すべり材のすべり板に当接されるすべり面がリング状に形成されることで、すべり摩擦を過剰に増大させることなくすべり材のすべり姿勢を安定化させることができるとともに、すべり材のすべりを阻害する異物がすべり面の内側へ侵入するのを防止することができる。

【0013】

また、請求項2では、請求項1の免震装置において、すべり板は円板形の本体部の周縁にすべり材側に突出されすべり材の滑動域を規制するすべり材用ストッパが設けられていることを特徴とする。

【0014】
この手段では、すべり板に滑動域を規制するすべり材用ストッパが設けられることで、すべり材がすべり板の本体部から離脱するのが阻止される。
【0015】
また、請求項3では、請求項1または2の免震装置において、すべり板が固定された上部構造物または下部構造部にすべり板のすべり材と反対側方向への弾性変形域を規制するすべり板用ストッパが設けられていることを特徴とする。
【0016】
この手段では、下部構造部に弾性変形域を規制するすべり板用ストッパが設けられることで、すべり板の必要以上の変形が阻止される。
【発明の効果】
【0017】
本発明に係る免震装置は、すべり支承構造を構成するすべり材に弾性を付与することで、すべり材自体に縦方向の震動に対する減衰機能を発揮させ、特許文献1に係る免震装置のガイド機構を不要にするため、横方向，縦方向の双方の震動に対して減衰機能を発揮することができて、設備コストが安価であるとともに大型の構造物に適用することがきる効果がある。また、すべり材のすべり板に当接されるすべり面がリング状に形成されることで、すべり摩擦を過剰に増大させることなくすべり材のすべり姿勢を安定化させることができるとともに、すべり材のすべりを阻害する異物がすべり面の内側へ侵入するのを防止することができるため、すべり支承構造による横方向の震動に対する減衰機能が円滑，確実に奏される効果がある。
【0018】
さらに、請求項2として、すべり板に滑動域を規制するすべり材用ストッパが設けられることで、すべり材がすべり板の本体部から離脱するのが阻止されるため、免震限界を超えた震動によって装置構成が簡単に崩壊することがなくなる効果がある。
【0019】
さらに、請求項3として、下部構造部に弾性変形域を規制するすべり板用ストッパが設けられることで、すべり板の必要以上の変形が阻止されるため、免震限界を

超えた震動によって装置構成が簡単に崩壊することがなくなる効果がある。
【図面の簡単な説明】
【0020】
【図1】本発明に係る免震装置を実施するための形態の縦断面図（要部拡大図を含む）である。
【図2】図1のX－X線断面図である。
【図3】図1の免震動作を示す図である。
【図4】図1の他の免震動作を示す図である。
【図5】図1のさらに他の免震動作を示す図である。
【発明を実施するための形態】
【0021】
以下、本発明に係る免震装置を実施するための形態を図面に基づいて説明する。
【0022】
この形態では、建屋の基礎付近に設備されるものを示してある。即ち、上部構造物Aとして建屋の柱体が対象とされ、下部構造物Bとして建屋の基礎体が対象とされている。
【0023】
この形態は、図1に示すように、上部構造物Aに固定されたすべり材1と下部構造物Bに固定されたすべり板2とからなるすべり支承構造を備えている。
【0024】
すべり材1は、上部構造物Aの下端部に固定され、上部構造物Aの下端部の外周面を覆う側壁面11の下部にリング状のすべり面12が設けられている（図2参照）。側壁面11は、すべり面12を上方から支持するとともに上部構造物Aの下端部を補強している。すべり面12は、断面形状が湾曲された形状に形成され、すべり板2に沿った円滑な滑動が得られるようになっている。すべり面12によって囲まれる底面に相当する非すべり面13は、上方に湾曲して凹入する形状に形成され、すべり面12を側方から支持するとともに上部構造物Aの底面部を補強している。
【0025】

すべり板2は、下部構造物Bに固定された支持ベース3に固定された支脚4に固定され、円板形の本体部21の周縁に上方（すべり材1側）に向けて突出されたすべり材用ストッパ22が設けられている。本体部21は、すべり材1のすべり面12よりも大きな径の円板形に形成され、中心部でのみ支脚4によって支持されて下部構造物B（支持ベース3）から少しのスペースを介するように立上げられている。この本体部21には、弾力が付与されており、上方（すべり材1側）に向けて中心部から凹状に湾曲するように付勢され非免震動作時に上部構造物Bの荷重で平板状（図1の状態）になるように弾性が設定されている。すべり材用ストッパ22は、すべり材1の滑動域を規制するもので、すべり材1がすべり板2の本体部21から離脱するのを阻止して、免震限界を超えた震動によって装置構成が簡単に崩壊しないようにする。

【0026】
これ等のすべり材1，すべり板2は、鋼材を主材として表面を耐腐食性，耐摩耗性を有するステンレス材とするとうの積層構造が選択される。なお、すべり材1，すべり板2の間では、すべり材1の円滑な滑動を奏するための平滑性が確保されるが、微小な震動ですべり材1が滑動しないようにある程度の摩擦係数が確保される。

【0027】
また、支持ベース3，支脚4は、鋼材を主材として形成される。なお、支持ベース3は、下部構造物Bに埋込み固定され、周縁にすべり板用ストッパ5が固定されている。すべり板用ストッパ5は、すべり板2の下方（すべり材1と反対側方向）への弾性変形域を規制するもので、すべり板2の必要以上の変形を阻止して、免震限界を超えた震動によって装置構成が簡単に崩壊しないようにする。

【0028】
この形態において地震等によって下部構造物Bが震動した場合には、図3に示すように、すべり板2の本体部21の上ですべり材1のすべり面12が滑動する（すべり支承構造）ことで、横方向の震動に対する減衰機能が発揮される。

【0029】
このすべり材1のすべり面12の滑動では、すべり面12がリング状に形成されているため、すべり摩擦を過剰に増大させることなくすべり材1のすべり姿勢を安

定化させることができるとともに、すべり材1のすべりを阻害する異物がすべり面12の内側へ侵入するのを防止することができる。この結果、すべり支承構造による横方向の震動に対する減衰機能が円滑，確実に奏されることになる。

【0030】
また、図4に示すように、上昇する下部構造物Bによってすべり材1のすべり面12に押圧されたすべり板2の本体部21が下方に向けて凹状に湾曲変形することで、縦方向（上方向）の震動に対する減衰機能が発揮される。

【0031】
また、図5に示すように、下降する下部構造物Bによってともに下降するすべり板2の本体部21が上方に向けて凹状に湾曲変形してすべり材1のすべり面12に対する押圧を維持することで、縦方向（下方向）の震動に対する減衰機能が発揮される。

【0032】
なお、横方向，縦方向の震動に対する減衰機能が発揮された後には、すべり板2の本体部21の弾力によって原位置（図1）への復元がなされる。

【0033】
従って、この形態によると、特許文献1に係る免震装置のガイド機構が不要になるにもかかわらず、横方向，縦方向の双方の震動に対して減衰機能を発揮することができる。この結果、構造が簡素化されて設備コストが安価になり、大きな荷重が掛かり細小な機構の付設が不向きな大型の構造物にも適用することがきるようになる。

【0034】
以上、図示した形態の外に、すべり材1，すべり板2の間に防塵シートを張設することも可能である。

【0035】
さらに、すべり板2のすべり材用ストッパ22やすべり板用ストッパ5に弾性を付与して、すべり材1，すべり板2を速やかに原位置に復元させるようにすることも可能である。

【産業上の利用可能性】

【0036】
　本発明に係る免震装置は、建屋以外の大型機械装置に設備して機械的振動の減衰にも強することが可能である。また、小型の構造物に適用しても何等支障のないものである。

【符号の説明】

【0037】

1	すべり材
12	すべり面
2	すべり板
21	本体部
22	すべり材用ストッパ
4	支脚
5	すべり板用ストッパ
A	上部構造物
B	下部構造物

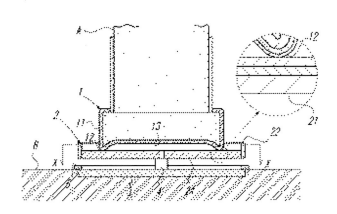

【図1】

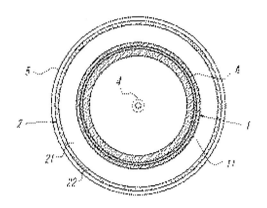

【図2】

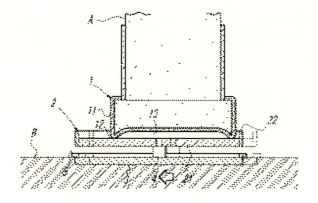

【図3】

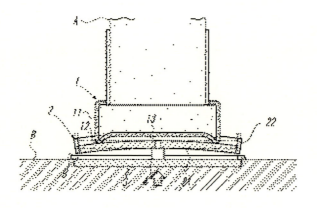

【図4】

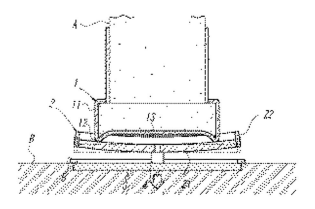

【図5】

4、
Patent journal English

[Claim 1]

In a base-isolating device provided with slide support structure by which slide material was fixed to one side of a superstructure and a substructure thing, and a bed slide was fixed to another side, A bed slide is energized so that it may curve from the central part to a concave towards slide material, it is formed by a plate material of a disk type with which elasticity was set up to become plate-like by load of a superstructure at the time of non-quake-absorbing operation, and is partially supported and fixed by leg only in the central part,A base-isolating device with which slide material is characterized by a sliding surface by which ring shape is abutted being provided by bed slide.

[Claim 2]

A base-isolating device, wherein a stopper for slide material which a bed slide is projected by periphery of a body part of a disk type at a slide material side, and restricts a sliding region of slide material in a base-isolating device of Claim 1 is provided.

[Claim 3]

A base-isolating device, wherein a stopper for bed slides which restricts an elastic deformation region to slide material and an opposite side direction of a bed slide in Claim 1 or a base-isolating device of 2 to a superstructure or a lower structure section to which a bed slide was fixed is provided.

DETAILED DESCRIPTION

[Detailed Description of the Invention]

[Field of the Invention]

[0001]

The present invention belongs to the technical field concerning the base-isolating device which decreases the shock (vibration) which is furnished between a superstructure and a substructure thing and it is transmitted from one side of a superstructure and a substructure thing to another side.

[Background of the Invention]

[0002]

As a base-isolating device, the thing provided with slide support structure has spread. Slide material is fixed to one side of a superstructure and a substructure thing, a bed slide is fixed to another side, and this base-isolating device is sliding slide material along with a bed slide, and decreases the shock which it is transmitted from one side of a superstructure and a substructure thing to another side.

[0003]

In this base-isolating device, there is the characteristic of hardly exhibiting a damping function to the shock of the longitudinal direction of what exhibits a damping function effectively to a lateral shock. For this reason, development of the technology in which a damping function is effectively exhibited also to the shock of a longitudinal direction in the base-isolating device provided with slide support structure is demanded.

[0004]

As technology which pointed to demonstrating a damping function effectively also to the shock of a longitudinal direction conventionally in the base-isolating device provided with slide support structure, the thing of the description to a Patent document 1 is known, for example.

[0005]

A bed slide is fixed to a superstructure by the Patent document 1, slide material is fixed to a substructure thing via the air spring of a bellows form, and the guide shaft which restricts the expansion and contraction direction of an air spring in a substructure thing, and the base-isolating device with which the guide mechanism which consists of linear bushing was attached are described in it.

[0006]

While the base-isolating device concerning a Patent document 1 demonstrates a damping function to the shock of a longitudinal direction with an air spring, the basic constitution of slide material and the slide support structure which consists of a bed slide is maintained, and the damping function to a lateral shock is kept from disappearing.

[Citation list]

[Patent literature]

[0007]

[Patent document 1] JP,H10-169708,A

[Summary of Invention]

[Problem to be solved by the invention]

[0008]

Since the attachment of a guide mechanism is needed in order to operate effectively the air spring which exhibits a damping function to the shock of a longitudinal direction in the base-isolating device concerning a Patent document 1, while structure will be complicated and facility cost will become high, big load is applied -- thin -- there is a problem of being inapplicable to a large-sized structure with an unsuitable attachment of a small mechanism.

[0009]

The present invention was made in consideration of such a problem, can exhibit a damping function to a shock of the both sides of a transverse direction and a longitudinal direction, and it makes it problem to provide a base-isolating device applicable to a large-sized structure while facility cost is inexpensive.

[Means for solving problem]

[0010]

In order to solve the above-mentioned problem, the base-isolating device concerning the present invention adopts the means of a description as each claim of Claims.

[0011]

Namely, in the base-isolating device provided with the slide support structure by which slide material was fixed to one side of a superstructure and a substructure thing, and the bed slide was fixed to another side in Claim 1, A bed slide is energized so that it may curve from the central part to a concave towards slide material, it is formed by the plate material of the disk type with which elasticity was set up to become plate-like by the load of a superstructure at the time of non-quake-absorbing operation, and is partially supported and fixed by the leg only in the central part,As for slide material, the sliding surface by which ring shape is abutted is provided by the bed slide.

[0012]

In this means, the slide material itself is made to exhibit the damping function to the shock of a longitudinal direction by giving elasticity to the slide material which constitutes slide support structure, and the guide mechanism of the base-isolating device concerning a Patent document 1 is made unnecessary. While being able to stabilize the slide attitude of slide material by the sliding surface by which the bed slide of slide material is abutted being formed in ring shape, without increasing sliding friction to an excess, the foreign matter which inhibits the slide of slide material can be prevented from entering into the inside of a sliding surface.

[0013]

In Claim 2, the stopper for slide material which a bed slide is projected by the periphery of the body part of a disk type at a slide material side, and restricts the sliding region of slide material is provided in the base-isolating device of Claim 1.

[0014]

In this means, it is prevented by the stopper for slide material which restricts a sliding region to a bed slide being provided that slide material secedes from the body part of a bed slide.

[0015]

In Claim 3, the stopper for bed slides which restricts the elastic deformation region to the slide material and opposite side direction of a bed slide to the superstructure or lower structure section to which the bed slide was fixed is provided in Claim 1 or the base-isolating device of 2.

[0016]

In this means, the deformation beyond the necessity for a bed slide is prevented by the stopper for bed slides which restricts an elastic deformation region to a lower structure section being provided.

[Effect of the Invention]

[0017]

The base-isolating device concerning the present invention is giving elasticity to the slide material which constitutes slide support structure, The slide material itself is made to exhibit the damping function to the shock of a longitudinal direction, and in order to make unnecessary the guide mechanism of the base-isolating device concerning a Patent document 1, a damping function can be exhibited to a shock of the both sides of a transverse direction and a longitudinal direction, and while facility cost is inexpensive, there is an effect which applying to a large-sized structure cuts. By what the sliding surface by which the bed slide of slide material is abutted is formed in ring shape for, While being able to stabilize the slide attitude of slide material, without increasing sliding friction to an excess, Since the foreign matter which inhibits the slide of slide material can be prevented from entering into the inside of a sliding surface, the damping function to the shock of the transverse direction by slide support structure has smoothness and the effect of being played reliably.

[0018]

Since it is prevented by the stopper for slide material which restricts a sliding region to a bed slide being provided as Claim 2 that slide material secedes from the body part of a bed slide, it is effective in it being lost that an equipment configuration collapses simply by the shock beyond a quake-absorbing limit.

[0019]

By the stopper for bed slides which restricts an elastic deformation region to a lower structure section being provided as Claim 3, since the deformation beyond the necessity for a bed slide is prevented, it is effective in it being lost that an equipment configuration collapses simply by the shock beyond a quake-absorbing limit.

[Brief Description of the Drawings]

[0020]

[Drawing 1]It is drawing of longitudinal section (an essential part enlarged drawing is included) of the form for carrying out the base-isolating device concerning the present invention.

[Drawing 2]It is a X-X line cross sectional view of Fig.1.

[Drawing 3]It is the figure showing quake-absorbing operation of Fig.1.

[Drawing 4]It is the figure showing quake-absorbing operation of everything but Fig.1.

[Drawing 5]It is the figure showing yet another quake-absorbing operation of Fig.1.

[Description of Embodiments]

[0021]

Hereinafter, the form for carrying out the base-isolating device concerning the present invention is described based on Drawings.

[0022]

This form has shown what is furnished near the foundation of a building. That is, the prism of a building is made into an object as the superstructure A, and let the basic field of the building be an object as the substructure thing B.

[0023]

This form is provided with the slide support structure which consists of the slide material 1 fixed to the superstructure A, and the bed slide 2 fixed to the substructure thing B as shown in Fig.1.

[0024]

The slide material 1 is fixed to the lower end part of the superstructure A, and the sliding surface 12 of ring shape is provided by the lower part of the side wall surface 11 which covers the outer peripheral surface of the lower end part of the superstructure A (refer to Fig.2). The side wall surface 11 has reinforced the lower end part of the superstructure A while supporting the sliding surface 12 from the upper part. The sliding surface 12 is formed in the form in which sectional shape curved, and smooth sliding which was along the bed slide 2 is obtained. The non-sliding surface 13 equivalent to the bottom surface surrounded by the sliding surface 12 curved up, was formed in the form which carries out a reentrant, and it has reinforced the bottom section of the superstructure A while it supports the sliding surface 12 from the side.

[0025]

The bed slide 2 is fixed to the leg 4 fixed to the supporting base 3 fixed to the substructure thing B, and the stopper 22 for slide material projected by the periphery of the body part 21 of a disk type towards the upper part (slide material 1 side) is provided. The body part 21 is formed in the disk type of a bigger path than the sliding surface 12 of the slide material 1, and it is started so that it may be supported by the leg 4 only in the central part and slight space may be passed from the substructure thing B (supporting base 3). Elasticity is given, and it is energized by this body part 21 so that it may curve from the central part to a concave towards the upper part (slide material 1 side), and elasticity is set to it to become plate-like (state of Fig.1) by the load of the superstructure B at the time of non-quake-absorbing operation. The stopper 22 for slide material restricts the sliding region of the slide material 1, and it prevents that the slide material 1

secedes from the body part 21 of the bed slide 2, and keeps an equipment configuration from collapsing simply by the shock beyond a quake-absorbing limit.
[0026]
the slide material 1, such as this, and the bed slide 2 use steel materials as a main material, and the laminated structure which will be obtained if the surface is used as the stainless material which has corrosion resistance and abrasion resistance is chosen. Although the smooth nature for playing smooth sliding of the slide material 1 is secured between the slide material 1 and the bed slide 2, a certain amount of coefficient of friction is secured so that the slide material 1 may not slide by minute shock.
[0027]
The supporting base 3 and the leg 4 are formed considering steel materials as a main material. The supporting base 3 is embedded and fixed to the substructure thing B, and the stopper 5 for bed slides is fixed to the periphery. The stopper 5 for bed slides restricts the elastic deformation region to the lower part (the slide material 1 and opposite side direction) of the bed slide 2, the deformation beyond the necessity for the bed slide 2 is prevented, and an equipment configuration is kept from collapsing simply by the shock beyond a quake-absorbing limit.
[0028]
When the substructure thing B shakes according to an earthquake etc. in this form, as shown in Fig.3, the damping function to a lateral shock is exhibited by what (slide support structure) the sliding surface 12 of the slide material 1 slides on on the body part 21 of the bed slide 2.
[0029]
Since the sliding surface 12 is formed [sliding of the sliding surface 12 of this slide material 1] in ring shape, while being able to stabilize the slide attitude of the slide material 1, without increasing sliding friction to an excess, The foreign matter which inhibits the slide of the slide material 1 can be prevented from entering into the inside of the sliding surface 12. As a result, it will be played smoothly [the damping function to the shock of the transverse direction by slide support structure], and certainly.

[0030]

As shown in Fig.4, the damping function to the shock of a longitudinal direction (above) is exhibited because the body part 21 of the bed slide 2 pressed by the sliding surface 12 of the slide material 1 turns caudad and carries out curved deformation to a concave with the substructure thing B going up.

[0031]

As shown in Fig.5, the damping function to the shock of a longitudinal direction (down) is exhibited by the body part 21 of the bed slide 2 which descends with both the descending substructure things B carrying out curved deformation to a concave towards the upper part, and maintaining the press to the sliding surface 12 of the slide material 1.

[0032]

After the damping function to the shock of a transverse direction and a longitudinal direction is exhibited, restoration to an original position (Fig.1) is made by the elasticity of the body part 21 of the bed slide 2.

[0033]

Therefore, although the guide mechanism of the base-isolating device concerning a Patent document 1 becomes unnecessary according to this form, a damping function can be exhibited to a shock of the both sides of a transverse direction and a longitudinal direction. as a result -- structure is simplified, facility cost becomes inexpensive and big load is applied -- thin -- it comes to cut that the attachment of a small mechanism applies also to an unsuitable large-sized structure.

[0034]

As mentioned above, it is also possible to carry out stretching of the dustproof sheet between the slide material 1 and the bed slide 2 out of the illustrated form.

[0035]

It is also possible to give elasticity to the stopper 22 for slide material and the stopper 5 for bed slides of the bed slide 2, and to make it restore the slide material 1 and the bed slide 2 to an original position promptly.

[Industrial applicability]

[0036]

The base-isolating device concerning the present invention can furnish heavy machinery equipment other than a building, and can carry out strong also to attenuation of mechanical oscillation. Even if it applies to a small structure, it is convenient in any way.

[Explanations of letters or numerals]

[0037]

1 Slide material

12 Sliding surface

2 Bed slide

21 Body part

22 The stopper for slide material

4 Leg

5 The stopper for bed slides

A Superstructure

B Substructure thing

* NOTICES *

JPO and INPIT are not responsible for any

damages caused by the use of this translation.

1.This document has been translated by computer. So the translation may not reflect the original precisely.

2.**** shows the word which can not be translated.

3.In the drawings, any words are not translated.

DRAWINGS

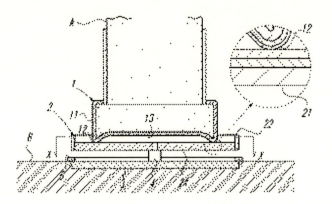

[Drawing 1]

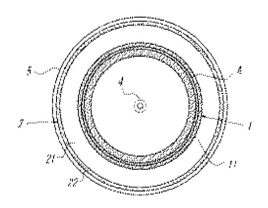

[Drawing 2]

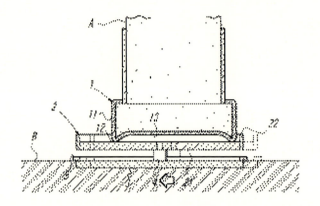

[Drawing 3]

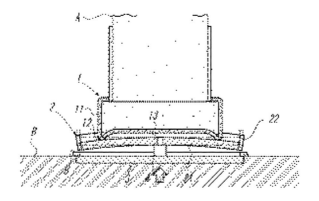

[Drawing 4]

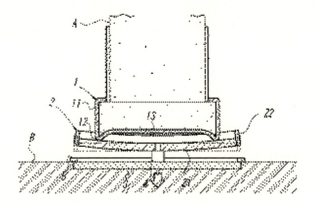

[Drawing 5]

本書の奥付の発行№.について

№.が記載された剥離紙が、枠内に貼られ角印が押されている。従って、これが複写された本書は、内容が異なる海賊版でありますからご注意ください。

About issue [of the colophon of this book] No.

The angle mark is stamped on the seal with which No. was indicated. Therefore, since this book with which this was copied is a pirate edition from which the contents differ, it should be careful.

定価（本体 1,800 円＋税）

２０１６年（平成２８年）１０月１７日発行

No.  SY99-8-068

発行所　IDF（INVENTION DEVLOPMENT FEDERATION）
　　　　発明開発連合会®

メール 03-3498@idf-0751.com　www.idf-0751.com

電話 03-3498-0751㈹

150-8691 渋谷郵便局私書箱第２５８号

発行人　ましば寿一

著作権企画　IDF 発明開発(連)

Printed in Japan

著者　佐山光男©

　　　（さやまみつお）

本書の一部または全部を無断で複写、複製、転載、データーファイル化することを禁じています。
It forbids a copy, a duplicate, reproduction, and forming a data file for some or all of this book without notice.